the perfect party

RICK RODGERS

ROMANTIC
DINNERS

Surefire recipes and exciting menus for a flawless party!

the perfect party

RICK RODGERS

ROMANTIC DINNERS

Surefire recipes and exciting menus for a flawless party!

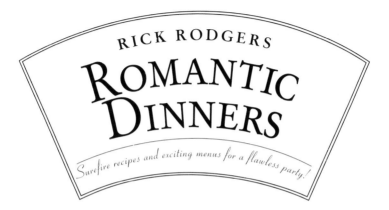

ILLUSTRATIONS BY ROBBIN GOURLEY

WARNER **W** TREASURES™

PUBLISHED BY WARNER BOOKS

A TIME WARNER COMPANY

Warner Treasures is a trademark of Warner Books, Inc.

Warner Books, Inc.
1271 Avenue of the Americas
New York, NY 10020

 A Time Warner Company

Book design by Robbin Gourley
Printed in Singapore
First Printing: March 1996
10 9 8 7 6 5 4 3 2 1

ISBN: 0-446-91095-3

CONTENTS

INTRODUCTION

"Cooking is like love. It should be entered into with abandon or not at all."

—Harriet Van Horne

EVER SINCE THE DAWN of time, people have been trying to prove that certain foods or beverages have the power to induce love. Although specific ingredients may not always live up to their reputation, it has been proved time and again that a fine meal can play an enormous role in lovemaking. Served at home rather than at a restaurant, a romantic dinner's intimacy is magnified. A sweet word, which would not be appropriate with a waiter or waitress nearby, can be whispered across your private dining-room table.

It is easy to see how food figures in the game of love. We toast our loved ones with a glass of Champagne or send them chocolates on Valentine's Day. When we have been separated from a lover, we celebrate the reunion with a special dinner. Physically speaking, this is no mistake; the same type of nerve endings that are found in the human mouth are also found in the sexual organs.

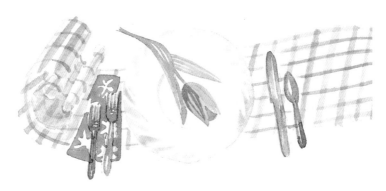

    This book offers a collection of menus that will help set the proper mood for fine dining and lovemaking. I have developed a wide range of dishes to cover a number of circumstances and tastes. So whether your special dinner must be a hearty one or a more delicate meal, you will be able to find just the right combination. For example, the first menu is created with a lady as guest of honor, and offers lightly flavored foods that make a lovely presentation. For dyed-in-the-wool carnivores, the second menu is a thick, juicy steak for a special occasion dinner. After the theater is a romantic time too, and in the third menu I include a quickly prepared supper created from some very special ingredients—ones that just happen to have unscientific reputations as aphrodisiacs. The book concludes with the luxury of breakfast in bed, a pleasure few of us savor enough, especially with a loved one by our side.

    Cooking for two is different from cooking for a party. Since the recipes in most cookbooks are for four to six servings, you would create a

mountain of leftovers if you followed these books. The recipes in this book call for just enough groceries for the special meal, and the preparations are done ahead as much as possible. After all, with love on your mind, you don't want to fuss with last-minute details. Every menu has a preparation timetable to help you organize your meal, in some cases days before the actual meal. In this busy age, my favorite recipes are those that give me the most flavor with the least effort. This book is filled with such dishes.

Of course, you can't rely on the food to do all of the work in romance. Be sure you have the lights dimmed for *l'amour* and candles on the table. (When you want to pull out all the stops, use candles in the living room too.) Set the table with your best china and most elegant tablecloth and napkins. Rather than arrange flowers in a vase, get a single rose and lay it at your guest's place. Load the CD player with romantic music—when in doubt, try classical guitar music, which many people find alluring without being stuffy.

9

The menus in this book share a common denominator—chocolate for dessert. Not only is chocolate likely to be a favorite of your guest's, it has a long tradition as an aphrodisiac. Chocolate was the love potion of the Aztec kings, and when it was brought to Europe, it was touted there also as a sexually stimulating beverage. Today we continue the tradition by giving chocolate candy as a love token, especially on Valentine's Day. Studies have suggested that a compound in chocolate, called phenylethylamine, is the same one that our brain produces during love's euphoria. Chocolate feels especially sensuous when eaten, one of the few foods with a melting temperature below our body's temperature, thus coating our mouths with a smooth, silky sweetness.

The actress Sophia Loren is certainly a contender for a modern-day Venus, the representation of both physical and romantic love. She gave us her secret for a triumphantly amorous meal: "The most indispensable ingredient of all good home cooking: love for those you are cooking for."

A ROMANTIC VALENTINE'S DAY DINNER

SHRIMP AND MANGO SALAD
WITH GINGER VINAIGRETTE

ROASTED CORNISH GAME HENS
WITH RICOTTA STUFFING AND NEW POTATOES

SAUTÉED GREEN BEANS
WITH PAN-ROASTED RED PEPPERS

California Chardonnay

CHOCOLATE-ORANGE SOUFFLÉ CAKES

Freshly Brewed Coffee or Tea

Grand Marnier

For 2 people

"There is no sight on earth more appealing than the sight of a woman making dinner for someone she loves."

—Thomas Wolfe

JUST BECAUSE YOU HAVE chosen to have your romantic St. Valentine's Day meal at home is no reason why the food has to be homely, in either a visual or emotional sense. The food that is most inviting combines the familiar and the contemporary, and is seasonally inspired and presented attractively.

This menu is not far removed from one you might have at an American-style bistro. Fresh ginger, which not long ago could be found only in Asian markets, is a flavor that has won many friends lately. Yet ginger is proof that there are few things truly new under the culinary sun. One of the most famous lovers of the past, Madame Du Barry, believed in its aphrodisiac powers and used it as a seduction tool, baking it into a soufflé. Here, the juice is extracted from the fresh root to make a zesty vinaigrette for a Shrimp and Mango Salad. Individual cornish hens are a great idea for dinners *à deux,* and these are baked with new potatoes, to provide two dishes from the same roasting pan. Sautéed Green Beans with Pan-Roasted Red Peppers makes a simple, colorful garnish to the main course. Freshly baked soufflés can be daunting, especially if the cook rushes to get them to the table without their falling. Even an old kitchen hand like myself doesn't want that kind of pressure during a romantic meal, but that doesn't mean soufflés have to be totally forgone. Unmold them to create Chocolate-Orange Soufflé Cakes, which can be served either warm or at room temperature, allowing the cook to buy as much time as needed.

PREPARATION TIMETABLE

Up to 2 days ahead:
♥ Make Ginger Vinaigrette for salad; cover and refrigerate.

Up to 1 day ahead:
♥ Prepare shrimp for salad; cover and refrigerate.

♥ Rinse watercress for salad; wrap in paper towels, store in a plastic bag; refrigerate.

♥ Parcook green beans; cool, cover, and refrigerate.

♥ Prepare orange segments for soufflé cakes; cover and refrigerate.

Up to 12 hours ahead:
♥ Prepare mango for salad; cover and refrigerate.

Up to 8 hours ahead:
♥ Make Ricotta Stuffing; cover and refrigerate.

Up to 4 hours ahead:
♥ Fills hens; cover and refrigerate.

About 2 hours before serving:
♥ Preheat oven; prepare potatoes; roast hens and potatoes.

♥ Pan-roast red peppers; store at room temperature.

About 1 hour before serving:
♥ Make chocolate base for soufflé cakes; store in a warm place.

♥ Prepare custard cups for soufflé cakes and place on a baking sheet.

About 20 minutes before serving:
♥ Complete Shrimp and Mango Salad; refrigerate.

When ready to serve:
♥ Remove hens and potatoes from oven and transfer to dinner plates; make sauce.

♥ Complete green beans; keep warm.

♥ Whip egg whites and fold into chocolate base; set timer for 20 minutes and bake soufflé cakes.

SHRIMP AND MANGO SALAD WITH GINGER VINAIGRETTE

Makes 2 servings

The combination of shrimp and mango is tasty and colorful. Dressed with the Ginger Vinaigrette, this combination makes a very refreshing salad. If you can't find ripe mangoes (they are at their peak in either late spring or early winter), use a ripe papaya instead.

Ginger Vinaigrette

1 tablespoon grated fresh ginger (use the large holes of a cheese grater)
2 tablespoons lime juice
2 tablespoons finely chopped red onion
1 teaspoon minced fresh hot green or red chile pepper, such as jalapeño
¼ teaspoon grated lime zest
¼ teaspoon minced garlic
¼ teaspoon salt
5 tablespoons olive oil

2 ripe medium mangoes, or 1 large ripe papaya
8 ounces medium shrimp
1 small bunch watercress, rinsed, tough stems removed
2 tablespoons chopped fresh mint or cilantro (optional)

1. Make the vinaigrette: Wrap grated ginger in the corner of a clean kitchen towel. Squeeze and wring

18

ginger over a medium bowl to extract juice; discard pulp. Add lime juice, red onion, chile pepper, lime zest, garlic, and salt; whisk well. Gradually whisk in oil. *The vinaigrette can be prepared up to 2 days ahead, covered, and refrigerated. Whisk to combine.*

2. Lay a mango on a work surface, plump side down. The mango pit is long and flat, and runs horizontally through the fruit, so the trick is to cut the flesh away without hitting the pit. Using a sharp, thin-bladed knife, slice off the top third of the mango, cutting around the pit. Turn mango over and slice off the other side. Repeat with the remaining mango. One piece at a time, using a large serving spoon, scoop out mango flesh in 1 piece from peel. Cut peeled mango pieces lengthwise into ½-inch-thick slices. (As the cook's treat, you can pare away the peel

from the pit, and nibble around it to get at the sweet mango flesh.) If using a papaya, peel, halve, scoop out the black seeds, and slice. *The mango can be prepared up to 12 hours ahead, covered, and refrigerated.*

3. Bring a medium saucepan of lightly salted water to a boil. Add shrimp and cook just until shrimp turn firm and pink, 2 to 3 minutes. Rinse well under cold running water. Peel and devein. *The shrimp can be prepared up to 1 day ahead, covered, and refrigerated.*

4. Place watercress in the center of 2 large plates. Top with shrimp. Fan the mango slices around both sides of the shrimp. Spoon the dressing on top of the salads and sprinkle with mint or cilantro, if desired. *The salad is best served immediately, but can be refrigerated for up to 20 minutes.*

ROASTED CORNISH GAME HENS WITH RICOTTA STUFFING AND NEW POTATOES

Makes 2 servings

An herb-scented cheese stuffing is a nice change from a heavy one made from all bread crumbs. The new potatoes are roasted right alongside the hens. To make the sauce, use a splash of the same white wine you are serving.

Stuffing

½ cup part-skim ricotta cheese
⅓ cup dried bread crumbs
¼ cup freshly grated Parmesan cheese
1 tablespoon chopped fresh basil or parsley
1 large egg yolk
1 garlic clove, crushed through a press
1 scallion, minced
⅛ teaspoon salt
⅛ teaspoon freshly ground pepper
Pinch of grated nutmeg

2 (1 pound each) Cornish game hens, rinsed and patted dry
¼ teaspoon plus ½ teaspoon salt
¼ teaspoon freshly ground pepper, divided
1 tablespoon plus 2 tablespoons olive oil
1 pound small new potatoes, scrubbed
⅓ cup dry white wine
1 tablespoon chopped fresh chives or parsley

1. Position rack in top third of oven and preheat to 350°F. Lightly oil a 9-by-13-inch flameproof baking dish, preferably nonstick.

2. In a medium bowl, combine all ingredients for stuffing. *The stuffing can be made up to 8 hours ahead, covered, and refrigerated.*

3. Season hens inside and out with ¼ teaspoon salt and ⅛ teaspoon pepper. Fill body cavities with stuffing. Using kitchen string, tie the

wings to the bodies, then tie the drumsticks together. Brush hens with 1 tablespoon oil. Place hens, breasts up, in prepared pan. *The hens can be stuffed up to 4 hours ahead, covered, and refrigerated.*

4. In a medium bowl, toss potatoes with remaining 2 tablespoons oil, ½ teaspoon salt, and ⅛ teaspoon pepper, coating potatoes completely with oil. Surround hens with potatoes.

5. Roast for 20 minutes. Stir potatoes, and turn hens onto one side, supporting the hens with the potatoes. Roast for another 20 minutes. Stir potatoes, then turn hens onto the opposite sides. Roast for 20 more minutes. Stir potatoes, and turn hens breast sides up. Roast until hens are golden brown and potatoes are golden brown and tender (a meat thermometer inserted in the thickest

part of the thigh not touching a drumstick will read 170°F.), about 30 more minutes. Total cooking time is about 1 hour, 30 minutes. Transfer hens and potatoes to warmed dinner plates.

6. Place baking dish over high heat on top of stove. Add wine and bring to a boil, scraping up browned bits on bottom of pan with a wooden spoon. Pour sauce over hens. Sprinkle hens and potatoes with chives or parsley and serve immediately.

SAUTÉED GREEN BEANS WITH PAN-ROASTED RED PEPPERS

Makes 2 servings

According to personal taste, other green vegetables can be cooked until crisp-tender and reheated with the red peppers—try asparagus spears, broccoli florets, zucchini slices, or sugar snap peas. If you can find them, use ultra-thin *haricots verts,* which will add an extravagant note to the proceedings.

6 ounces green beans, trimmed
1 tablespoon olive oil
½ medium sweet red pepper, seeded and cut into ½-inch cubes
⅛ teaspoon salt
⅛ teaspoon freshly ground pepper
1 tablespoon balsamic vinegar

1. Bring a medium saucepan of lightly salted water to a boil over high heat. Add green beans, return to the boil, and cook until crisp-tender, about 2 minutes. Drain, rinse well under cold water, and drain again. *The green beans can be prepared up to 1 day ahead, stored in a plastic bag, and refrigerated.*

2. In a medium skillet, preferably nonstick, heat oil over medium heat. Add red pepper. Cover and cook until red pepper is tender and lightly browned, about 5 minutes. *The red pepper can be prepared up to 2 hours ahead, kept in the skillet, and held at room temperature. When ready to serve, reheat the red pepper over medium heat, stirring occasionally, until sizzling.*

3. Add green beans, salt, and pepper. Cook, stirring often, until green beans are heated through, about 3 minutes. Sprinkle with balsamic vinegar and serve immediately.

CHOCOLATE-ORANGE
SOUFFLÉ CAKES

Makes 2 servings

In French, *soufflé* means a breath or a sigh (a lover's sigh?). These baked confections are so named for their ethereal, light-as-air quality. The pleasure in serving a soufflé is to rush it to the table while it is still dramatically puffed, for it will fall very soon after removing from the oven. But these chocolate soufflés are *supposed* to fall. Unmolded onto plates, they become warm, melt-in-your-mouth cakes that garner sighs of appreciation. You will need two large Pyrex custard cups to make these individual cakes, easily found at kitchenware stores or even supermarkets.

¼ cup plus 1 tablespoon granulated sugar
1 tablespoon cornstarch
⅛ teaspoon salt
½ cup milk
2 ounces high-quality bittersweet chocolate, such as Lindt Excellence, finely chopped
1 tablespoon unsalted butter, at room temperature
1 large egg, separated, plus 1 large egg white, at room temperature
½ teaspoon grated orange zest
1 tablespoon orange-flavored liqueur, such as Grand Marnier, or orange juice
½ teaspoon vanilla extract
Confectioners' sugar, for dusting
1 large navel orange, peeled, cut between membranes into individual segments, chilled

1. Position a rack in the center of the oven and preheat to 400°F. Butter inside of two 300 ml (1¼ cups) custard cups and sprinkle with 1 tablespoon sugar, tapping out excess

sugar. Place prepared custard cups on a baking sheet.

2. In a small saucepan, combine cornstarch, remaining ¼ cup sugar, and salt. Gradually whisk in milk to dissolve cornstarch. Cook, whisking often, over low heat, until thickened and simmering. Remove from heat. Add chocolate and butter. Let stand for 3 minutes, then whisk until smooth and melted. Whisk in egg yolk, orange zest, Grand Marnier or orange juice, and vanilla. *The soufflé can be prepared up to this point 2 hours ahead of time. Place a buttered round of waxed paper directly on the surface of the chocolate mixture and let stand in a warm place. The mixture must be warm, but not hot, before proceeding. Cook very gently over low heat, stirring constantly, if necessary, to reheat.*

3. In a medium, grease-free bowl, using a handheld mixer set at medium-high speed, beat egg whites until stiff, but not dry. Stir about one-fourth of the whites into chocolate mixture to lighten. Transfer mixture to bowl of remaining egg whites. Using a rubber spatula, fold until combined. Transfer to the prepared ramekins.

4. Bake until soufflés are puffed and a toothpick inserted in center comes out clean, about 20 minutes. Remove from oven and let stand for 5 minutes.

5. Run a knife around insides of custard cups to release. Invert onto dessert plates and unmold. Sift confectioners' sugar over plates and soufflé cakes to dust completely. Arrange orange segments in a pinwheel pattern on top of each cake. Serve warm.

A CANDLELIGHT DINNER FOR A
MEAT-AND-POTATOES LOVER

GREEN SALAD WITH GORGONZOLA TOASTS

GRILLED STEAKS
WITH MUSHROOM–RED WINE COMPOTE

PESTO TWICE-BAKED POTATOES

Cabernet Sauvignon or Zinfandel

VANILLA ICE CREAM
WITH CHOCOLATE-COGNAC SAUCE

Freshly Brewed Coffee or Tea

Cognac

For 2 people

"The way to a man's heart is through his stomach."

—Fanny Fern

WHILE LOVE FOR YOUR guest is certainly an important part of a good meal, that is only part of the story. It is also important to stay within your basic cooking skills; don't try to show off with fancy tricks that may not work. When under pressure to serve a romantic meal, there's nothing wrong with sticking with what you know. The key element is that these recipes are easy to pull off, so even the inexperienced cook can approach this meal with confidence.

It's the same when you decide what to serve. If your guest loves meat and potatoes, go with that and make the person happy. He or she can have grilled fish and salad some other night. Remember, many men love to grill and to eat grilled foods. This is a simple fact—don't mess with it. (The grilled dishes in this menu can also be broiled indoors.)

Green Salad with Gorgonzola Toasts starts the meal off with an intriguing combination of hot and cold temperatures. Grilled Steak is served

31

with a rich Mushroom–Red Wine Compote, but don't worry that the compote will need last-minute attention—it can be made well ahead of time and reheated. Pesto-Twice Baked Potatoes couldn't be easier, but they couldn't be better, either. And dessert is your favorite store-bought ice cream gilded with homemade Chocolate-Cognac Sauce.

PREPARATION TIMETABLE

Up to 1 day ahead:
♥ Make vinaigrette; cover and refrigerate.

Up to 4 hours ahead:
♥ Make Mushroom–Red Wine Compote.
♥ Make chocolate sauce; store at room temperature.

Up to 2 hours ahead:
♥ Bake potatoes for Pesto Twice-Baked Potatoes; make filling; fill potatoes; store at room temperature.
♥ Toast bread, spread with blue cheese; store at room temperature.

About 45 minutes before serving:
♥ Light charcoal grill or preheat gas grill.

About 20 minutes before serving:
♥ Complete baking of potatoes.

When ready to serve:
♥ Grill bread slices; dress salad and top with toasts.
♥ Grill steaks; transfer to plates.
♥ Reheat compote and serve with steaks.
♥ Just before serving, scoop ice cream and top with sauce.

GREEN SALAD WITH GORGONZOLA TOASTS

Makes 2 servings

Use any blue cheese you prefer—Italian Gorgonzola, French Roquefort, Danish or American blue, or English Stilton. Or if you or your guest aren't blue cheese fans, simply serve the toasted croutons plain, perhaps rubbed with a garlic clove, if you both agree.

Vinaigrette

1 tablespoon minced shallot or scallion
2 teaspoons red wine vinegar
2 teaspoons balsamic vinegar
⅛ teaspoon salt
6 tablespoons extra-virgin olive oil

4 slices French or Italian bread (about ⅓ inch thick)
2 ounces blue-veined cheese, at room temperature
1 medium head Boston lettuce, torn into bite-size pieces
Freshly ground pepper to taste

1. Make the vinaigrette: In a small bowl, whisk shallot, red and balsamic vinegars, and salt. Gradually whisk in olive oil. *The vinaigrette can be prepared up to 1 day ahead, covered, and refrigerated. If necessary, whisk again until smooth.*

34

2. Position the broiler rack 4 inches from the source of heat and preheat broiler (see Note). Broil bread, turning once, until lightly toasted on both sides. Spread with blue cheese. *The bread slices can be prepared up to 2 hours ahead and stored at room temperature.*

3. When ready to serve, toss lettuce with vinaigrette. Transfer to chilled plates. Broil cheese-topped bread until cheese is melted and bubbling, about 1 minute. Place 2 toasts on top of each salad. Serve immediately with a peppermill so each guest can add pepper as they choose.

Note: The toasts can also be prepared on a charcoal or gas grill. Grill toasts over medium-high coals (or medium-high heat) until toasted on one side. Spread toasted sides with softened cheese. Place on the grill,

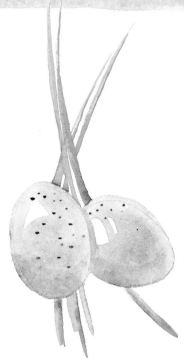

untoasted side down, and cover with the grill lid. If using a charcoal grill, place the toasts around the cooler, outside edges of the grill, not directly over the coals. Grill until the cheese is melted, about 3 minutes.

GRILLED STEAKS WITH MUSHROOM—RED WINE COMPOTE

Makes 2 servings

These steaks can certainly be broiled or pan-fried, if you prefer. Well-aged steaks from a good butcher will make your dinner extra-special. Depending on the part of the country you live in, the same cut will be called sirloin, sirloin strip, shell steak, or New York steak. The intensely flavored compote is the perfect partner for the grilled steak. To make the compote, use some of the red wine you have chosen to serve with your steak.

Mushroom—Red Wine Compote

3 tablespoons unsalted butter, divided
1 small onion, cut into ¼-inch-thick half-moons
6 ounces fresh mushrooms, thinly sliced
½ cup dry red wine
½ cup beef stock, preferably unsalted homemade, or use reduced-sodium canned broth
¼ teaspoon dried thyme
⅛ teaspoon freshly ground pepper
Salt to taste

2 (14- to 16-ounce each) sirloin steaks, cut about 1 inch thick
2 teaspoons olive oil
Salt and freshly ground pepper to taste
1 tablespoon chopped fresh parsley, for garnish

1. Make the mushroom compote: In a medium skillet, heat 1½ tablespoons butter over medium heat.

Add onion. Cover and cook, stirring occasionally, until onion is golden brown, about 7 minutes. Transfer to a plate and set aside.

2. Add remaining butter to skillet and heat. Add mushrooms. Cook, stirring occasionally, until mushrooms have given off their liquid, it evaporates, and mushrooms are lightly browned. Add red wine, beef broth, thyme, and pepper. Increase heat to high and boil until liquid has almost completely evaporated, about 5 minutes. Season with salt. *The compote can be prepared up to 4 hours ahead and stored at room temperature. Reheat over medium heat.*

3. Meanwhile, build a hot charcoal fire in an outdoor grill. Let the coals burn until completely coated with white ash. Rub both sides of steak with oil. Place steaks on grill and cover with grill lid. Cook, turning once, until steaks are cooked to desired doneness, about 9 minutes for medium-rare, or longer, if desired (see Note.) The steak can also be prepared in a preheated broiler with the rack positioned 4 inches from the source of heat.

4. Transfer steaks to dinner plates and season with salt and pepper. Divide mushroom compote between plates and sprinkle with parsley. Serve immediately.

Note: There is an easy way to test steak's doneness without cutting into the meat. Press the steak in the center. If it feels soft, it is rare to medium-rare. If it is somewhat firm, the steak is medium. A well-done steak feels firm and resilient.

PESTO TWICE-BAKED POTATOES

Makes 2 servings

Pesto and Parmesan cheese make a delicious variation on the twice-baked potato theme.

1 large (9 ounces) baking potato, such as russet or Idaho, well scrubbed
2 tablespoons sour cream or plain yogurt
2 tablespoons prepared pesto
Salt and freshly ground pepper to taste
1 tablespoon freshly grated imported Parmesan cheese
1 teaspoon olive oil

1. Position a rack in the top third of the oven and preheat to 375°F. Place the potato directly on the rack and bake until tender, about 1 hour.

2. Cut hot potato in half lengthwise (protect your hand from the heat with a kitchen towel). Using a large spoon, scoop out potato flesh into a bowl, leaving ¼-inch-thick shells. Add sour cream and pesto and coarsely mash potato flesh. Season with salt and pepper to taste. Spoon mixture into potato shells and place on a baking sheet. Sprinkle with Parmesan cheese and drizzle with oil. *The potatoes are best if baked and served immediately, however they can be prepared up to 2 hours ahead, covered, and stored at room temperature.*

3. Bake until potatoes are golden brown, 15 to 20 minutes. Serve hot.

VANILLA ICE CREAM WITH CHOCOLATE-COGNAC SAUCE

Makes 2 servings

This luscious warm chocolate sauce hardens where it comes in contact with the frozen ice cream to make a dessert of intriguing textures and temperatures. If you prefer a liquid sauce, delete the butter and increase the heavy cream to ¼ cup. You may use other spirits to substitute for the cognac, or try brewed coffee, if you prefer to leave out the alcohol. Fresh berries in season can be added as fillip.

Chocolate-Cognac Sauce

2 tablespoons water
2 tablespoons heavy cream
2 tablespoons unsalted butter
1 tablespoon light corn syrup
4 ounces semisweet chocolate, finely chopped
1 tablespoon Cognac or brandy

1 pint vanilla ice cream
Fresh raspberries or sliced strawberries, for garnish (optional)

1. Make the chocolate sauce: In a small saucepan, bring water, cream, butter, and corn syrup to a simmer over low heat, stirring to melt butter. Remove from heat. Add chocolate and Cognac. Let stand for 3 minutes, then whisk until smooth and melted. *The chocolate sauce can be prepared up to 4 hours ahead and stored in a warm place. If desired, reheat over*

low heat, stirring constantly, just until warm. Do not allow sauce to come to a simmer.

2. Scoop ice cream into dessert bowls or wine glasses. Pour sauce over ice cream, add berries, if desired, and serve immediately.

AN EXTRAVAGANT AND
ELEGANT LATE-NIGHT SUPPER

ROASTED OYSTERS WITH TOMATO-LIME SALSA

FRESH LINGUINE WITH CAVIAR AND CRÈME FRAÎCHE

BELGIAN ENDIVE, WATERCRESS, AND WALNUT SALAD

Champagne

CHOCOLATE AND RASPBERRY POTS DE CRÈME

Freshly Brewed Coffee or Tea

Port Wine

For 2 people

"There is more simplicity in the man who eats caviar on impulse than in the man who eats Grape-Nuts on principle."

—G. K. Chesterton

SO MANY FOODS HAVE been labeled aphrodisiacs that it is almost easier to make a list of those that have not been so honored. As a group, foods of the sea have been more likely nominees. This is probably because Venus was goddess of both the sea and love. Her birth from sea foam is often depicted with the goddess on a seashell, so it's possible seafood got its reputation by this association.

This is a seafood dinner that can be tossed together in less than thirty minutes. It is perfect for a late-night supper after a concert or the theater, when you want to be able to serve without delay. As soon as you walk in the door, turn on the oven to preheat and put on water to boil the pasta. Have you ever noticed that some of the most expensive foods need the least attention? At this supper, the first course is the ready-in-a-flash Roasted Oysters with Tomato-Lime Salsa. The main dish couldn't be more luxurious—Fresh Linguine with Caviar and Crème Fraîche—with a Belgian Endive, Watercress, and Walnut Salad served alongside. Earlier in the day, or even the day before, Chocolate and Raspberry Pots de Crème have been made and are sitting in the refrigerator ready to be a midnight indulgence. Champagne, the lovers' beverage, is a perfect accompaniment to the supper.

PREPARATION TIMETABLE

Up to 10 days ahead:
♥ Make crème fraîche, if using homemade.

Up to 1 day ahead:
♥ Make Tomato-Lime Salsa.
♥ Make glazed walnuts for salad; cool and chop; store at room temperature.
♥ Make vinaigrette for salad; cover and refrigerate.
♥ Make pots de crème; cover and refrigerate.

Up to 12 hours ahead:
♥ Prepare endive and watercress for salad; wrap in paper towels and store in a plastic bag; refrigerate.

Up to 30 minutes ahead:
♥ Preheat oven.
♥ Bring water to boil for pasta.

When ready to serve:
♥ Roast oysters; top with salsa.
♥ Complete salad.
♥ Prepare linguine with caviar.

Just before serving:
♥ Top pots de crème with whipped cream.

ROASTED OYSTERS WITH TOMATO-LIME SALSA

Makes 2 servings

If you can find a cooperative fishmonger to open the oysters (or if you are skilled enough to do it yourself), you can serve them on the half shell. However, I like the ease of roasting, and most of my guests prefer the flavor and texture of the lightly cooked version. Either method benefits from a spicy, sharp condiment such as this fresh salsa. Outside of tomato season, use imported Holland or Israeli tomatoes.

Tomato-Lime Salsa

1 large ripe tomato
2 tablespoons lime juice
1 tablespoon minced red onion
2 teaspoons minced fresh cilantro (optional)
2 teaspoons minced fresh hot green chile pepper (such as jalapeño)
¼ teaspoon minced garlic
⅛ teaspoon salt

12 fresh oysters

1. Make the salsa: Bring a medium saucepan of water to a boil over high heat. Add tomato and cook for 30 seconds. Drain and rinse under cold running water. Using a small sharp knife, peel and cut in half horizontally. Squeeze tomato halves gently to remove seeds. Chop tomato finely and transfer to a small bowl. Stir in remaining ingredients. Cover and refrigerate until well chilled, at least

1 hour. *The salsa can be prepared up to 1 day ahead, covered, and refrigerated.*

2. Preheat the oven to 500°F. Place the oysters on a baking sheet and bake just until opened, about 3 to 5 minutes.

3. Arrange oysters on 2 large plates. Place a spoonful of salsa on each oyster and serve immediately.

FRESH LINGUINE WITH CAVIAR AND CRÈME FRAÎCHE

Makes 2 servings

My local caviar source carries four varieties: beluga, osestra, sevruga, and American (black or golden sturgeon or red salmon caviar). They all have their positive features, so let your budget guide your choice. (Let me warn you that beluga, which has the largest eggs and whose rarity makes it the most expensive, has a subtle flavor that may be lost when paired with the pasta, so unless you are a dedicated enthusiast, or rich, buy one of the other varieties.) Please note that we are discussing fresh caviar, not dyed lumpfish eggs, which are not nearly good enough to share with a loved one at a special meal. One caveat: be sure your bowls are warmed before adding the pasta, or it may cool off too quickly. Either warm the bowls in a 200°F. oven for about 5 minutes, or place the bowls in the sink and pour some of the hot pasta cooking water into them as you drain the linguine. Let the water stand in the bowls until you are ready to fill them.

9 ounces fresh linguine
½ cup crème fraîche or sour cream (see Note)
2 ounces caviar
Freshly ground pepper to taste

1. Bring a large pot of lightly salted water to a boil over high heat. Add linguine and cook just until tender, about 2 minutes. Do not overcook. Drain well, and return pasta to the pot.

2. Reduce heat to low. Add crème fraîche and stir until it melts and

coats the pasta, about 1 minute. Transfer to 2 warmed bowls and top with caviar. Serve immediately with a peppermill so you can season as you wish.

Note: Crème fraîche is available in the dairy or cheese departments of many specialty grocers. It is similar to sour cream, but a little less tangy. To make your own crème fraîche, whisk 1 cup heavy cream (preferably not ultra-pasteurized) with 1 tablespoon buttermilk or sour cream in a small bowl. Cover loosely with plastic wrap. Let stand in a warm place (near the stove or a water heater) until thickened like sour cream, which can take 24 to 48 hours, depending on the weather. Refrigerate overnight. The crème fraîche will keep up to 10 days, covered and refrigerated.

BELGIAN ENDIVE, WATERCRESS, AND WALNUT SALAD

Makes 2 servings

Belgian endive is one of the most labor-intensive vegetables grown, causing it to be one of the pricier salad greens. Harvested completely by hand, the heads are planted and replanted a number of times to give the vegetable its unique pale color, slightly acrid flavor, and crisp-tender texture. Watercress has a milder bite and adds a splash of color. The glazed walnuts temper the greens' bitterness and add crunch. This is a very special salad for a very special guest.

1½ tablespoons Champagne or white wine vinegar
⅛ teaspoon salt
⅛ teaspoon freshly ground pepper
6 tablespoons French walnut oil or extra-virgin olive oil
3 tablespoons sugar
1 tablespoon water
⅓ cup walnuts
1 head Belgian endive, cored and cut crosswise into ¼-inch-thick rings
1 cup watercress leaves (without stems)

1. In a small bowl, whisk vinegar, salt, and pepper. Whisk in olive oil in a steady stream. *The dressing can be prepared up to 1 day ahead, covered, and refrigerated. If necessary, whisk again to combine.*

2. In a small bowl, stir sugar and water until combined. Place walnuts and sugar mixture in a small nonstick skillet and stir over

medium-low heat until the liquid comes to a simmer. Cook without stirring, but swirling the skillet occasionally by the handle, until the syrup is golden brown, about 2 minutes. Pour out onto a lightly oiled piece of foil. Separate nuts with 2 forks and cool completely. Using a sharp knife, coarsely chop the glazed walnuts and set aside. *The walnuts can be prepared up to 1 day ahead, stored at room temperature.*

3. In a medium bowl, toss endive and watercress with dressing. Transfer to chilled plates and sprinkle with chopped glazed walnuts. Serve immediately.

CHOCOLATE AND RASPBERRY POTS DE CRÈME

Makes 2 servings

Chocolate and raspberries is one of my favorite combinations. I have nibbled the bottoms out of an entire box of chocolates, searching for the one with the raspberry cream filling. Pots de crème are like individual mousses, but are richer in deep, dark chocolate flavor and also denser. You can serve these in ramekins, but I prefer using martini glasses for a more fun presentation.

4 ounces high-quality bittersweet chocolate, such as Lindt Excellence, finely chopped
1 large egg yolk
½ cup milk, heated
1 tablespoon raspberry-flavored liqueur, such as Chambord, or seedless raspberry preserves
½ cup fresh raspberries
Sweetened whipped cream, for garnish
Additional raspberries, for garnish

1. Place chocolate in a small bowl and set aside.

2. Place egg yolk in a small saucepan. Gradually whisk in milk. Cook over low heat, stirring constantly, just until thick enough to coat a wooden spoon, about 2 minutes. Pour over chocolate and add liqueur. Let stand 3 minutes, then whisk until completely smooth.

3. Divide raspberries between two 6-ounce ramekins or large martini glasses. Spoon chocolate mixture over berries and smooth tops. Cover with plastic wrap and refrigerate until well chilled, at least 2 hours.

The desserts can be prepared up to 1 day ahead, covered, and refrigerated.

4. Garnish each with a dollop of whipped cream and a few raspberries. Serve chilled.

BREAKFAST IN BED FOR TWO

SCRAMBLED EGGS WITH SMOKED SALMON (OR HAM)
AND HERBS

FRESH BAKED BAGELS OR CROISSANTS*

PAPAYA AND BERRIES WITH CHAMPAGNE AND HONEY

Freshly Brewed Coffee or Tea

Freshly Squeezed Orange Juice

Champagne

For 2 people

*Recipe not included

"A simple enough pleasure, surely, to have breakfast alone with one's husband, but how seldom married people in the midst of life achieve it."

—Anne Morrow Lindbergh

THE EVERYDAY BREAKFAST is hardly the time for a romantic meal, when nobody is at his or her best, rushing out to catch the train or worrying about that morning meeting. But Mrs. Lindbergh had the right idea—when a weekend breakfast for the two of you is made into a special occasion, it can be very special indeed.

Again, simplicity is the secret here. Don't make anything too complicated. Breakfast in bed is even better when it is presented as a surprise to your loved one, and lots of banging around in the kitchen will give the secret away. Serve something that is easy to eat propped up in bed. Scrambled Eggs with Smoked Salmon (or Ham) and Herbs is perfect. (Pancakes or waffles, dripping with syrup and melted butter, is not.) You'll need a breakfast bread like bagels or croissants, so run out to the local bakery to pick them up. (Either can be purchased ahead of time, frozen, and left out overnight to defrost.) Brightly colored and flavored Papaya and Berries with Champagne and Honey is a welcome eye-opener.

A standing bed tray is an important implement, and two trays are even better. This meal can be served on lap trays. I like to keep the fruit separate from the eggs, so if you want them on the same plate for ease in serving, put the fruit in a small bowl so the dressing doesn't run into the eggs. If you plan to serve jam or jelly with the bread, put it into a small serving pot with its own spreading knife, which will cut down on sticky fingers—one of the banes of an improperly served breakfast in bed. Butter the bread, if desired, before you bring it to the bedroom, so you don't have to juggle the butter dish, too. If you are sure of how your lover likes either coffee or tea, prepare it in the cup and leave the sugar bowl and creamer in the kitchen. In other words, streamline. The less you bring into the bedroom, the less that can get spilled.

Two elements always make breakfast in bed just that much more of a treat: freshly squeezed orange juice and Champagne. Champagne gets splashed into the fruit as a dressing, and while I choose to keep it out of my orange juice, you can pour it into your juice glass to make a mimosa. And, above all, don't neglect to set a fresh rose in a bud vase on the tray. It will say "good morning" and "I love you" at the same time.

PREPARATION TIMETABLE

The night before:
♥ Chop herbs and salmon for eggs; cover and refrigerate.
♥ Drizzle papaya and berries with honey; cover and refrigerate.
♥ Chill Champagne.

About 20 minutes before serving:
♥ Brew coffee or tea.
♥ Squeeze oranges for juice.

Just before serving:
♥ Toast bagels or heat croissants.
♥ Scramble eggs.
♥ Pour Champagne over fruit.

SCRAMBLED EGGS WITH SMOKED SALMON (OR HAM) AND HERBS

M a k e s   2   s e r v i n g s

In New York, where I live, smoked salmon is *de rigueur* for a special breakfast. In other parts of the country, however, ham is considered equally necessary, and can easily replace the salmon. With salmon-flecked eggs, I would naturally serve toasted bagels, but I opt for croissants if offering ham and eggs. Gentle cooking ensures delicate, tender eggs. Don't season the eggs until after cooking, as different kinds of smoked salmon or ham will supply varying amounts of salt.

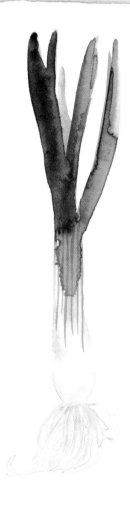

5 large eggs
3 tablespoons heavy cream
2 tablespoons unsalted butter
2 ounces thinly sliced smoked salmon or ham, finely chopped
1 tablespoon chopped fresh parsley
1 tablespoon chopped fresh chives or scallion
1 teaspoon chopped fresh tarragon, or ¼ teaspoon dried
Salt and freshly ground pepper to taste

1. In a medium bowl, whisk eggs and cream. In a medium skillet, preferably nonstick, heat butter over medium-low heat. Add eggs and cook, stirring often, until beginning to set but still quite liquid, about 2 minutes.

2. Add smoked salmon or ham, parsley, chives, and tarragon and continue cooking until cooked to desired doneness, about 1 minute more for

soft-scrambled eggs. Season with salt and pepper. Transfer to 2 warmed plates; serve immediately.

PAPAYA AND BERRIES WITH CHAMPAGNE AND HONEY

Makes 2 servings

Splash a bit of the Champagne you are serving over the honey-drizzled fruit to add a touch of elegance to a simple fruit salad.

1 ripe papaya, peeled, seeded, and cut into wedges
1 cup fresh berries (raspberries, blueberries, blackberries, or sliced strawberries)
2 tablespoons honey
¼ cup Champagne
Fresh mint sprigs, for garnish (optional)

1. In a medium bowl, drizzle papaya and raspberries with honey and fold gently. Cover tightly and refrigerate until well chilled, at least 1 hour. *The fruit can be prepared up to 12 hours ahead, covered, and refrigerated.*

2. Spoon fruit into 2 chilled bowls. Divide Champagne over fruit and stir gently to dissolve honey. Garnish with mint sprigs, if desired, and serve immediately.